Guaranteed Formula for

Effective Meeting Facilitation

&

Participation

- by Everett Ofori, MBA (UK), MSF (USA)

10-digit ISBN: 1-894221-08-7
13-digit ISBN: 978-1-894221-08-5

Other Books by Everett Ofori

1) Succeeding From the Margins of Canadian Society: A Strategic Resource for New Immigrants, Refugees and International Students. Written by Francis Adu-Febiri and Everett Ofori© 2009 – ISBN 978-1-926585-27-7

2) Read Assure: Guaranteed Formula for Reading Success with Phonics. © 2010 – ISBN 978-1894221054

3) Guaranteed Formula for Writing Success. © 2019 – ISBN 978-1-926918-22-8

4) The Changing Japanese Woman: From Yamatonadeshiko to YamatonadeGucci   © 2013 – ISBN 13: 978-1894221047

5) Prepare for Greatness: How to Make Your Success Inevitable. © 2013 – ISBN 13: 978-0921143000

6) The Global Student's Companion: 10,001 Timeless Themes & Topics for Dialogue, Discussion & Debate Practice. Compiled by Everett Ofori   © 2015 – ISBN 13: 978-1-894221-02-3

7) Guaranteed Formula for Effective Business Writing. © 2011 – ISBN 978-1894221108

8) Guaranteed Formula for Public Speaking Success. © 2011 – ISBN 978-1894221078

9) 3,570 Real-world English Phrases for Speaking & Writing Practice (Volume 1) © 2011 – ISBN 978-1894221125

10) 3,570 Real-world English Phrases for Speaking & Writing Practice (Volume 2) © 2011 – ISBN 978-1894221139

11) 3,570 Real-world English Phrases for Speaking & Writing Practice (Volume 2) © 2018 – ISBN 978-1894221160

Preface

Whether you are the leader of a group or a member of a team, the quality of your communication determines, to a great extent, how influential you are. If you consistently demonstrate the ability to think and share your thoughts, as well at intelligently question the status quo without alienating those around you, it won't be long before you find yourself donning the leadership mantle. Some people are born with the proverbial "gift of the gab," but anyone with strong determination can learn to be the kind of communicator that commands attention both by the content of what he or she says and by how the message is delivered.

The techniques presented in this book will help the reader to learn not only some of the technical aspects of leading or participating in a meeting but also how to do so in a way that gets respect. Anyone can express an opinion, but expressing an opinion that takes into consideration facts and reality, and questions assumptions that many others take for granted, requires courage.

Formal versus Informal Language

In general, the world of business is less formal today than it was in the past. Slang words and expressions that are overly informal are sometimes unsuitable for business situations. At the same time, expressions that are too formal may not fit. Formal expressions often use long words and sentences and words that are not always so common. If you read good quality newspapers and magazines, you would not have to worry about being too informal. An informal expression like "Let's go get a bite" is quite common and acceptable even in business situations, especially where the parties have gotten to know each other.

"Meetings are at the heart of an effective organization, and each meeting is an opportunity to clarify issues, set new directions, sharpen focus, create alignment, and move objectives forward."

- Paul Axtell, Communications Consultant, USA

UNIT 1
How to Use This Book

The book has been designed not just to present theory, but to give users realistic practice opportunities. Each section begins with brief notes, and ends with a practice session.

Having anywhere from three to seven participants can work; having a larger group may mean less talking time for some participants. It should be the goal of participants to master not only how to effectively facilitate a meeting but also be a good participant. A meeting attendee who says nothing will not be of much benefit to the group.

As with most things in life, those who try hard to apply the information are the ones who will most benefit from it. But mechanically following the steps outlined is also not the goal. As the great management guru, Dr. Peter Drucker wrote, "Follow effective action with quiet reflection. From the quiet reflection will come even more effective action." In other words, think about what you learn, and consider how and where best to use the ideas. If there is an instructor leading the class, they can let participants read short sections of the text, ensure that they understand, explain any parts that are not crystal clear, and then get the participants to practice what they are learning.

The instructor should ensure that everyone gets the chance to practice what is the focus of a particular unit. And everyone should get the opportunity to play the role of facilitator as well as a contributing participant. After covering mini-presentations, if the class is two hours long, one half could be devoted to mini-presentations and the other half to meetings/discussions. This can bring in some variety to the class.

UNIT 2
Giving an Opinion

While you may be eager to know the views of others at a meeting, soon enough you will have to share your own opinions. There are a number of isgnals or cues that you can use to show that you are about to share an opinion. The most common cue, perhaps, is "I think..."

Here are some of those useful signals:

In my opinion...	In my view...
I'd say...	I suppose...
I believe that...	If you ask me...
The way I see it...	It's a fact that...
My view is that...	It seems to me that...
Nobody will deny that...	I think that...
I feel that...	It seems that...
As far as I'm concerned...	From my point of view...
I'm of the opinion that...	As I see it...

The above are useful for expressing opinions. These are opinions that you may not feel so strongly about. They may simply be an observation you have made.

Even so, your tone of voice can also play a part in how others interpret what you have said. So, pay attention to your tone because it can convey strong belief, irritation, excitement, or even lack of interest.

Practice:

Let's try using some cues to express opinions about the following topics:

For example,

TOPIC/ISSUE	CUE/SIGNAL
Christmas in Japan	**In my view**, Christmas in Japan is all about illumination.
Cyberbullying	**In my opinion**, social media platforms should act faster in removing comments that appear to bully others.

Practice expressing opinions on each of the following. Use any of the signals on the previous page.

1) Team building	7) Transportation network
2) Motivation	8) Importance of design
3) Performance appraisals	9) Internet speed
4) Goal setting	10) Smartphones
5) Leadership	11) Learning English
6) Conflict resolution	12) Exercising for health

UNIT 3
Expressing Strong Conviction

When you feel strongly about something, you often want to make it known. How strongly you feel about an issue can sway other members to your point of view. Of course, it helps if what you are saying is grounded in facts.

Here are a few cues to help you express STRONG CONVICTIONS.

1) I certainly think that...	7) It's very clear to me that...	13) I have a strong conviction that...
2) I'm certain that...	8) I'm firmly convinced that...	14) There's absolutely no question...
3) I feel strongly that...	9) I'm absolutely convinced that...	15) It's crystal clear to me that...
4) It's quite clear that...	10) There can be no doubt that...	16) As everyone knows...
5) It's my firm belief that...	11) It's a fact that...	17) It is generally accepted that...
6) I firmly believe that...	12) I strongly believe that...	18) It's common knowledge that...

What do you feel strongly about?

I certainly think that_____

_____

I strongly believe that_____

_____

I feel strongly that...

_____

I have a strong conviction that_____

_____

It is my considered opinion that_____

_____

You can also use the following phrases to express preference for something:

Expressing Preference
- For my part, it would be useful to...
- I prefer X to Y
- It would be preferable for me if...
- I would rather...than...
- It seems to me that X has the following advantage -
- The reason I am partial to X is...
- My reason for supporting X is...

Practice using some of the above phrases to make sentences of your own.

1. _____

_____

_____

2. _____

_____

_____

3. _____

_____

_____

Practice: Try using different phrases/signals from the previous page to express strong convictions about the following.

1) Videogames	4) Long working hours	7) Amusement parks
2) Body piercing	5) Promotion	8) Tipping
3) Pets	6) Zoos	9) Gun control

UNIT 4
Expressing Tentative Opinions

Some people respond better to opinions that are expressed in a tentative way because it gives the listener an opportunity to think for himself or herself and decide whether to support the view. When you express a very strong view, unfortunately, you may turn off some people. On the other hand, expressing the opinion tentatively may give others the chance to chime in, and together, come to a decision that reflects the will of the group rather than one person.

Here are some useful phrases for expressing tentative opinons.

> * It's perhaps only fair to say that...
> * One might say that...
> * It seems to me that...
> * I would say that...
> * As far as I'm able to judge...

Practice: Express your opinion about these topics: it can be neutral, strong, or tentative. You may use signals from the previous units as well.

1) College education	4) Shopping	7) Social media
2) Private schools	5) Travelling	8) Telephone sales
3) Reading books	6) Golfing	9) Visiting the hospital

UNIT 5
Providing An Explanation

After expressing your opinion, other members at a meeting might want to know why you took that position. You don't want to keep everybody guessing. You owe the other members an explanation.

Logic in Business

The study of logic is very exciting for mathematicians. But logic in business is not a matter of mathematics. In business, logical argument is a matter of giving good reasons why you agree or disagree with a proposal. Your job is to think — and to offer your company the benefit of your thinking, which may come in the form of opinions, reasons, and supporting facts and figures

Avoid Circular Reasoning

- The media is good because it is the best!

- The local transportation system is good because I love it!

- This product is great because no other product is as good.

Where are the *real* reasons for making the **POINT** that you made?

To convince your colleagues of the value of your ideas, you need to give solid reasons. This is why preparation is essential. Take time before the meeting to think through the issues that will be discussed. You are then much more likely to come up with good, solid **REASONS** for the choices you make. If you want people to really understand what you are saying, give an **EXAMPLE**. Or tell a brief STORY that illustrates the point that you want to share. Finally, some people talk and talk and talk but end up saying nothing of substance. Try not to be that kind of person.

To back up your opinions with some reasons and to present the information in an elegant way, you ca use the following framework: PREP.

P: Point

R: Reason(s)

E: Example

P: Point

Model

Neighborcation

Point: *I think* it's a good idea for people to take a vacation in their own neighborhoods.

Reason: *This is because* in everyday life, many people ignore things around them, so they may not have paid attention to the gems in their own neighborhood.

Example: *For example*, during the 2020 coronavirus pandemic, I got tired of staying at home all the time. At the same time, the government encouraged us not to be out and about so much so that we could reduce the rate of infection. I found a charming little busines s hotel in my neighborhood and checked in for two weeks. I did not have to worry about cooking or cleaning. I was able to work from the hotel room with a feeling of renewed energy.

Point: *So, I encourage* everyone to explore what is in your own neighborhood, and take full advantage of them. It would be good for you, and your neighbors will love you for it.

Providing an Explanation - Giving Reasons

The simplest way of giving an example is to use the phrase "For example, ..." or "For instance,..."

Here are some other cues or signals you may use at the beginning of your explanation.

Let's consider...	Well, the thing is...
What I mean is...	The main problem is...
The reason I take this position is...	We should keep in mind that...
Let me explain...	Let me give an example...
The reason for this is...	The reason is that...
This is why...	I base my argument on...
(I support government bailouts) **because**....	Here's the deal...

MODEL:

Let's combine GIVING AN OPINION and PROVIDING AN EXPLANATION. The first one has been done for you. Try your hand at the others.

TOPIC/ISSUE		
FREE PUBLICITY		
Point	P	**As I see it**, it makes a lot of sense for us to seek free publicity for our services...
Reason	R	**Let me explain...**In the last few years the number of information outlets has exploded and many of these are looking for products and services to talk about.
Example/Story	E	**For example**, there are sites such as Craigslist that allow anyone to advertise for free. More than that, I am thinking about blogs and newsletters that focus on some of the same products and programs we market. If we give free samples of our products to prominent bloggers and newsletter editors, we stand a good chance of getting some free publicity.
Point	P	What I am trying to say is that before we spend thousands of dollars on marketing and advertising, we should seriously consider getting to know prominent bloggers and explore how we can use them to make our products better known to consumers. **Free publicity, I am sure you will all agree, is the most cost effective way to appeal to the public.**

The final point (P) does not need to be the same words as the initial point. You can express the same idea using different words. Getting back to the theme of your initial topic will signal to the participants that you have come to the end of your comment and that it's time for someone else to pick up from there.

Practice

Why not try using PREP to share your opinion, reasons and examples on the following topics:

TOPIC/ISSUE		
360° EVALUATION		
Point	P	
Reason	R	
Example/Story	E	
Point	P	

TOPIC/ISSUE		
FLEX WORK SCHEDULE		
Point	P	
Reason	R	
Example/Story	E	
Point	P	

TOPIC/ISSUE		
ONLINE TRAINING		
Point	P	
Reason	R	
Example/Story	E	
Point	P	

TOPIC/ISSUE		
ELECTRIC VEHICLES		
Point	P	
Reason	R	
Example/Story	E	
Point	P	

TOPIC/ISSUE		CUE
CORPORATE ENTERTAINMENT		
Point	P	
Reason	R	
Example/Story	E	
Point	P	

OTHER TOPICS FOR PREP PRACTICE

- Face masks

- Working overtime

- OJT: On the Job training

- Twitter marketing

- 3D Printers

- Gift giving

UNIT 6
Agreeing with an Opinion

When it comes to agreeing with someone, there is no shortage of cues we can give. Sometimes, our nonverbal cues indicate our agreement, like nodding our head. But you can use any of the phrases below to clearly show that you agree with someone.

I agree	That's right.
That's true.	That's it. You're right.
That's just how I feel about it.	That's exactly how I feel.
That's precisely what I think.	That's precisely how I feel.
That's a good point.	That's a pretty good point.
That's a very good point.	That's just the way I see it.
How true.	How very true.
I couldn't agree more.	I completely agree.
I fully agree.	I'm of the same opinion.
I have to say I agree with you on this...	You make a very good point.

Phrases for PARTIAL AGREEMENT

- I agree to a certain extent, but...
- You may be right, but have you considered....
- Yes. On the other hand....
- I agree with you but only up to a point...
- Yes, possibly...Although.....
- Yes, it depends....
- Yes, but there's another aspect to consider...

Practice

How much do you agree with each of the following? Provide support for why you agree or disagree. (You may use PREP)

1. The whole world should use the same currency.

2. Taxes should not be more than 5% of one's salary.

3. Graffiti should be taught in school.

4. Watching movies is a better way to learn than reading books.

5. Every child should have a mobile phone.

6. Employees should be able to choose their office hours.

7. The only success that counts is one that puts money in your bank account.

8. Shopping online is safer than shopping in person.

9. Grammar is a pain in the neck.

10. Self-driving cars are the future.

UNIT 7
Expressing Disagreement

What do you do when someone says something and you think it's wrong. What do you say? Even though we do not want to be rude to others, there are times when we are obliged to speak up and express our disagreement. For example, your boss has told you that some business partners that are coming to visit you are allergic to seafood. You want to entertain them well. Your boss is out of town, and you and other colleagues are tasked with choosing a restaurant where you would take the coming visitors. Someone has suggested that you take the visitors to a seafood restaurant because it is the most classy place in the neighborhood. You cannot simply agree to it. All your colleagues love seafood and see the occasion as an opportunity to indulge themselves. In such a case, you cannot passively allow the others to make the decision. You know certainly that your boss will not be happy with you if you do not make her viewpoint known - in the strongest possible terms.

Disagreeing with an opinion

I'm not sure...	I'm not so sure about that...	You don't mean that, do you...
I'm not quite convinced that...	I don't think that's right....	I don't want to argue but...
I doubt very much that...	Are you suggesting that...	I'm not so certain about that...
I have reservations about that...	I don't think it's quite as you put it...	I don't think it's like that at all...
I'm not sure what to make of that...	I can't go all the way with you on that...	I wonder if you've considered the alternative of..

I beg to differ on that...	You may be right, however...	Don't you think another method might be....
I don't quite agree there...	Another idea might be...	I can't accept the view that...
I disagree completely...	Well, that's one way of looking at it, but...	It's not as simple as that...
I doubt that very much....	I'm afraid I can't agree with you on that...	On the contrary...

Practice:

How much do you agree or disagree with each of the following? make use of any of the signals above. (You may use PREP)

1. Every car should have a breathalyzer.

2. The use of seat belts should be optional.

3. Nuclear power is the key to the world's energy needs.

4. Soy sauce should be banned from the dinner table.

5. Big cars should be banned.

6. Computer programming should be a required subject in school.

7. Cars do more harm than good.

8. Women make better leaders than men.

9. Cell phones should be banned in restaurants.

10. Cash will soon be obsolete.

UNIT 8
Enumerating / Listing

Do you sometimes listen to interviews of politicians, business people, artists, writers, and other prominent professionals.

If so, you may have noticed that some of the most impressive communicators are those who use enumeration techniques.

For example, "I have three reasons for saying that..." is more impressive than "I have some reasons for saying that..."

Once again, if you are well prepared and have given enough thought to the points you seek to express, it may be considerably easier to share your thoughts using enumeration.

Some useful phrases,

- First of all...
- To begin with...
- Firstly, ...Secondly..., Thirdly,...Finally.....
- In the first place...Second...
- For starters....
- For a start...
- To start with...
- One point I want to make is...Another point is....
- Let me give you two reasons for that....
- Let me share with you three quick points...

Practice: Use enumeration to comment on each of the following topics. As each other questions to expand the discussion.

Workplace bullying

Favoritism

Promotions

Privacy

UNIT 9
Extending the Discussion

Many issues you might discuss in a meeting are not so simplistic. They may have many different aspects to them. This means that after stating your initial position, you might not be able to stop there.

You might need to extend the point by adding other points or by highlighting exceptions to what you have already said. You might also have to shift from the topic at hand to temporarily consider another related matter.

Raising a New Point
- Let's now consider...
- Shall we turn now to the issue of...
- The next point we have to consider is...
- We can not ignore the matter of...
- Turning to another issue...

Making an Additional Point
- Additionally...
- In addition...
- Not only...but also...
- Moreover...
- Furthermore...
- I might add that...
- We cannot foreget the other point that...
- As well as...there is also...

Expressing Pros and Cons

- There are two sides to this question: One is...The other is...
- On the one hand...On the other hand...
- An argument for...is...
- Some people believe that....Others think that...
- One argument in favor of X is....but...

Model

1) *I believe that* bus service in this city is not given enough attention by the government. *In addition*, the government is beginning to reduce the budget for train service. This means that in a few years, the transportation system could totally fall apart.

2) My supervisor has rejected every report I have ever submitted. *Moreover*, she has stated that my ideas are not welcome, whether they are good for the company or not. It may be time for me to transfer to a new division.

Practice: Make sentences

Additionally...

_____

_____

_____

In addition...

_____

_____

Not only...but also...

_____

_____

_____

Moreover...

_____

_____

_____

Furthermore...

_____

_____

_____

Practice: Showing Contrast Between Two Ideas

On the one hand...but, on the other hand...

_____

_____

_____

In spite of...I think...

_____

_____

_____

Although...it is important to understand that...

_____

_____

_____

Despite the fact that...

_____

_____

_____

One might suppose that...but in reality...

_____

_____

_____

Practice: Generalizing

In general...

_____

_____

_____

All in all...

_____

_____

_____

On the whole...

_____

_____

_____

All things considered...

_____

_____

_____

Looking at the big picture...

_____

_____

_____

Practice: Stating Preference

I prefer A to B because...

_____

_____

_____

I would rather... than....for the simple reason that...

_____

_____

_____

...has an advantage over...in that....

_____

_____

_____

The main advantage of....is that...

_____

_____

_____

Between A and B, there is no question that for me, A...

_____

_____

_____

Practice

Share your opinions with one another. Try to use as many of the signal as possible, including making additional points, stating a preference, enumerating, etc.

1. Martial arts

2. Tourism

3. Sumo wrestling

4. Karaoke

5. Climate change

6. Animal testing

7. Mentors

8. Poor location for a business

9. Poor financial management

10. Succession planning

UNIT 10
Confirmation & Complaints

Even though all participants at a meeting might strive to speak as clearly as possible, this does not mean that everyone will always be understood the first time around. Sometimes, participants have to check with the speaker if what they are hearing is right. Thus, confirming or complaining should not be seen as negative. They help to make matters clear.

Confirming

- Do you mean that...
- You mean....right?
- You said that...Is that a fact?

Model

1. Do you mean that **everyone will get to go on the trip?**

2. **You mean** that I can take charge of the group, **right**?

3. **You said tha**t 40% of senior managers in Japan are women. **Is that a fact?**

Practice

Do you mean that_____

_____

_____

You mean_____

_____

_____right?

You said that_____

_____

_____Is that a fact?

Asking for a reaction

I wonder how you feel about...	Could ask what you think about ...
I was wondering where you stood on the question of....	Could I ask for your reaction on...

Model (Make your own sentences below)

1. **I wonder how you feel about** the recent increase in consumption tax.

2. **I was wondering where you stood on the question of** opening an overseas branch next year.

3. **Could I ask what you think about** the recent bribery scandal in the local government?

4. **Could I ask for your reaction on** the collusion between Company A and Company B?

5. _____

_____

6. _____

_____

7. _____

_____

Making a Complaint (Make some sentences below)

- I can't quite understand how...
- I'm disappointed to hear that...
- I'm sorry to have to say that....
- Are you aware that...
- Can you believe that...

1. _____

_____

2. _____

_____

3. _____

_____

4. _____

_____

5. _____

_____

6. _____

_____

Reacting to a Complaint

- I'm sorry to hear that...
- I must apologize for this...
- I'll see what I can do...
- Is that right? I'll look into it...
- What can I do to remedy the situation?
- I can't believe that happened. So sorry....

Practice (Roleplay)
How would you respond to the following complaints while a meeting is going on?

1. Madam Chairman, I never received a copy of the agenda beforehand. I understand everyone got it yesterday.

----

2. Mr. XXXXXX, every time I try to say something, you interrupt me. I don't particularly appreciate that.

----

3. Ms. XXXXXXX, as head of the events committee, I was hoping that you would take the lead in our negotiations with hotels, but it seems you let the junior staff do this, and now we are stuck with paying a very high amount for our upcoming series of events.

----

4. Mr. Chairman, it seems you are giving all the talking time to the ladies. Will you allow the men to say anything?

----

5. Ms. XXXXX, it seems that you're not following up fast enough on issues we present to your office. As such, a lot of work has backed up and if that continues, I'm afraid we're going to have a very poor quarterly result.

UNIT 11
Role of Meetings

If people can communicate by email or by phone or in person and get what they need done, there would be no need for face-to face meetings. Meetings, however, are necessary if getting people together is really the most effective way to accomplish something. Meetings usually involve two or more people coming together for any number of reasons. For example,

Solve a problem	Seek an answer to an external threat	Assign work
Negotiate a contract	Share information	Explore new options
Seek common ground	Seek opinions	Make decisions on an urgent matter
Resolve intergroup conflict or differences of opinion	Report on individual or group work	Chart a path for the future

Part of the role of the chairperson is to ensure that the goal of the meeting is achieved. Thus, the chairperson will ensure that all the items on an agenda are discussed within the time set aside for them. If there are items that require voting on, the chairperson will make sure that a full discussion takes place. At a point in the meeting where no fresh ideas are coming forward, the chairperson may decide to put the question to a vote or announce what decision he or she has come to if the chairperson has the ultimate power to make such decisions.

Discussion

1) In your own organization, what are some reasons for attending meetings?

2) What are some examples of meetings that you feel are unnecessary?

Practice: **How much do you agree or disagree with each of the following? Give reasons, and emphasize the main point you want to make. After someone expresses an opinion, the others should try to ask some follow-up questions.**

1. The voting age should be reduced to 15.

2. Gift exchange events among employees should be held monthly.

3. . Plastic grocery bags should be banned.

4. Money is the most important thing in the world.

5. Selfishness is a virtue.

6. Greed is good.

7. It is not a good idea to take risks.

8. We should always say hello to people we see in an elevator.

9. Revenge is the best way to deal with disrespectful people.

10. Everyone should be encouraged to eat whale meat.

UNIT 12
Love Attending Meetings?

Have you ever heard someone say, "I love attending business meetings!" Maybe not. Most people do not attend meetings out of love. Many people attend meetings because it is part of their job to do so. Meetings make it possible to share information, or to seek input, or signal that a new policy is important.

Whether you like meetings or not, they are quite likely a part of your life as a businessperson.

While some companies have come to the conclusion that meetings are a waste of time, we could take the position that meetings are only a waste if they are not run well. With proper attention to a few details, meetings can become an effective means of achieving company goals and become a joy to attend whether you are the chairperson or a participant.

Discussion practice. Express your opinion on a topic. Other participants will agree or disagree. Try to come to a conclusion on what most people think about the subject.

1. Living in a big city

2. Long working hours

3. Onsen (hot springs)

4. Earthquake warnings

5. School clubs

6. Business role models

7. Japanese business style

8. The importance of hierarchy in business

9. E-books have taken over the world.

10. Your pet peeves

UNIT 13
The Joy of Meetings

Psychologists often say that you cannot change what you do not acknowledge. So, a good starting point for turning loathsome meetings into joyful, productive gatherings is to acknowledge what each person might dislike about meetings. A few have been listed below, but you may have a few of your own that are not mentioned below.

Common Complaints about Meetings

- Holding meetings when the telephone or email could have served the same purpose
- Little or no preparation before the meeting
- No agenda
- Poor time management
- Poor meeting management and facilitation
- Poor handling of conflict
- Distractions by latecomers
- Useless interruptions
- Lack of follow-through on action items

Discussion

1) What do you particularly dislike about turning meetings?

2) What have you always wanted to see at meetings but seldom see?

UNIT 14
Emphasizing a Point

If you are responding to a question, or expressing your opinion and find the need to draw attention to what is important, you can use any of the following phrases:

It's important for us to know that...	We need to think about...	Let me repeat...
You need to consider that...	It is important that...	Let me make it clear...
You need to know...	One key factor is....	Let me explain...
You need to remember that...	Please take note...	A basic fact is that...
We need to take into consideration...	Let me emphasize that...	

Examples

After reading the examples below, use some of the phrases above to form your own sentences.

1. **It is important for us to know that** we can succeed in this project only if we support each other.

2. **You need to know that** I'm prepared to give this project 110%.

3. **We need to take into consideration** all the different types of clients we are trying to serve.

4. **We need to take into consideration that** compensation is based on effort and results.

5. It is important that we acknowledge our shortcomings and try to improve upon our performance.

6. _____

_____

_____

7. _____

_____

_____

8. _____

_____

_____

9. _____

_____

_____

Practice

Discuss the topics below. As you do so, try to use some of the above signals to emphasizd points that you really want others to pay attention to.

1. Ecotourism

2. Fast food restaurants

3. Gender diversity

4. Airline safety

5. Medical marijuana

6. Tax havens

7. Cryptocurrencies

8. Terrorism

9. Mental health

10. Luxury products

UNIT 15
Before the Meeting

Meetings do not happen by accident. Someone usually has a good reason to call one. Of course, some meetings are routine, as for example, a meeting of sales staff every Wednesday morning. Other meetings are called because there is an important issue that requires discussion and decision.

If you are responsible for setting up a meeting, you want to make sure that you have chosen a date and time that is convenient for those invited to attend.

Participants should know where the meeting is going to take place, the venue.

Some time before the meeting, you will want to share this information. Such advance notice of the theme of the meeting can be useful in the sense that it could encourage potential participants to prepare for it.

If you are going to be the discussion leader or chairperson of the meeting, you will need to prepare an agenda or ensure that you designate someone to prepare the agenda.

Discussion

1) What else can you think of that the facilitator can do before the meeting to help make the meeting run smoothly?

UNIT 16
The Agenda

You get notice that there is going to be a meeting. You have a rough idea of what the meeting is going to be about. Maybe, it's a meeting about new sales promotion strategies, or perhaps, one about the company's budget for the upcoming year.

If you don't know what a meeting is going to be about, it is difficult to prepare well. Once at the meeting, it is possible that you may be able to participate because of your knowledge and experience but having advanced knowledge of the theme may make you come prepared -- by thinking more about the issue, talking to other knowledgeable people, or by doing some research. There is no question that when you come prepared you will be more comfortable participating and perhaps be in a better position to make a meaningful contribution.

If you are the one calling the meeting, the sooner you begin working on the agenda, the better. A couple of weeks before the meeting, you can prepare a tentative agenda, a rough list of items you are considering for discussion.

When the agenda is prepared well ahead of the actual time of the meeting or conference, you also have more time to make changes and to get input from other potential participants or key figures within the organization before the meeting.

Having an agenda	Not having an Agenda
- guides you through the meeting - helps you keep time - helps you run a professional meeting	a meeting can be: - disorganized - time consuming - a waste of time

Practice: Some of these topics provide you with an opportunity to express strong disagreement. Whether you agree or not, be prepared to give reasons for the position you take.

1. Everyone should read at least one book a month.

2. Coffee is a dangerous drink.

3. Fast food is not fast enough.

4. Snake soup should be on the menu of every school.

5. Earthquake drills are a waste of time.

6. An annual beauty contest should be held for business women.

7. The government should force companies to build kindergartens for their employees' children.

8. Nurses are overpaid.

9. No one should learn a second language.

10. Cats and dogs should never live in the same house.

UNIT 17
Preparing an Agenda

I f you are the one calling the meeting or one assigned to create an agenda, begin by listing in bullet-point form the items that you expect participants in the meeting to discuss. Ask potential participants if there are any issues they want to bring up for discussion. Some of the points they mention may already be on your list. Add any new ideas that you consider important.

Type up the agenda and distribute it to those expected to attend the meeting. On the day of the meeting, make sure you have a few extra copies on hand in case someone forgets to bring his or her agenda.

If the meeting is a routine meeting, one that is held regularly, then it's a good idea to begin the agenda with a reading of the minutes of the last meeting. This reminds attendees of what took place at the previous meeting and helps lead in to what is expected at the current meeting. If it's a special meeting with no connection to a previous meeting, then you do not have to worry about previous minutes.

It is always a good idea to choose someone to write down the minutes of the meeting. This person is the scribe or secretary and it has to be someone who is comfortable writing quickly and accurately.

Before the meeting, make sure that each participant is aware of his or her role. This information can be on the agenda and distributed to the attendees before the meeting or you can let participants know directly or through email what they are expected to do. This can help such participants prepare, and thus, contribute more meaningfully to the meeting

Discussion

1) What is your personal view about the use of an agenda?

2) In what situation might an agenda not be so useful?

UNIT 18
An Effective Agenda

To create an effective agenda,, you might want to consider the following:

Purpose of the Meeting

Think about why a meeting is being called. What is the goal of the meeting? You may include information on who will attend, and who the facilitator will be.

Time Management

Set a time-frame for the meeting: start and end time. You may also break down the meeting by indicating how much time you will set aside for different issues. Alternatively, if participants have been asked to speak on particular issues, let them know how much time they have to do so.

Flexibility

If you are in charge of running the meeting, remind participants of the importance of sticking to time. At the same time, good judgment suggests that you have to be flexible. If you realize that a little more time devoted to an important issue will lead to a useful outcome, go for it.

Focus

It is very easy for a discussion to shift to unrelated matters. If you're the facilitator, help participants get back on track.

Record/Minutes

You may keep track of major decisions by writing them down on a board so all participants can see them. This approach can also be useful to the person taking the minutes as the individual can more clearly identify what is important enough to note down and what might be a minor point that can be ignored.

Writing Space

Meeting attendees may bring paper or notebooks upon which they will jot down ideas and points made at the meeting. You can leave space on the agenda for this purpose as well. This will be useful for those, who for one reason or another, find themselves without a writing pad, notepad, iPad, or laptop.

Practice

1. Executive coaching

2. Effective sales teams

3. Workplace stress

4. Resolving conflict

5. The art of persuasion

6. How to Take Criticism

7. Big meetings

8. Gamification

9. Building consumer awareness

10. The importance of diversity

UNIT 19
Agenda Samples

Here are three samples of very simple, straightforward agendas. As you can see, an agenda doesn't have to be any fancy.

MATSUBARA TRADING INC.

April 12, 2015

At 7-11-X Kita Shinjuku, Tokyo, Japan
Head Office

New Media Marketing Meeting No. 1

1. Apologies
2. Chairperson's welcome
3. Minutes of the last meeting
4. Unfinished business
5. Marketing manager's report
6. CFO's report
7. New media strategy discussion

8. Date, time, and venue for next meeting

MATSUBARA TRADING INC.

May 17, 2016

At 7-11-X Kita Shinjuku, Tokyo, Japan
Head Office

Time: 1:30 pm

Monthly meeting – Business Development Group

1:30 pm	Roll call
1:35	Previous minutes
1:55	
	Reports
	Finance
	Accounting
	Marketing
	Public relations
2:30 pm	Old business
2:45	New business
3:00	Adjournment

MATSUBARA TRADING INC.

July 28, 2017

At 7-11-X Kita Shinjuku, Tokyo, Japan
Head Office

1. Introduction of participants
2. Purpose of the meeting
3. Project review
4. Market analysis report
5. Suggestions and recommendations

6. Date and time for next meeting

Practice

Imagine that you are going to be the facilitator for the next meeting in your company. Create what you believe might be a realisting agenda. Be sure to have a listing of five to seven items for this assignment.

Agenda

UNIT 20
Mini Presentations at Meetings

The kind of presentation you have to do at a meeting is usually not a long one. Sometimes, you will get to do it sitting down. In other cases, you will do it while standing. Yet another option is for you to stand at a lectern prepared for the occasion so that you can give your presentation.

Your presentation may or may not involve the use of technology such as a projector. The range of options is quite wide. It depends on what kind of organization you are working for, what kinds of issues you routinely deal with, and what the expectations are within your company.

In any case, if there is any chance that you will be called upon to speak, it would make sense for you to go in well prepared. As the legendary American public speaking instructor, Dale Carnegie, wrote,

> "Only the prepared speaker deserves to be confident."

But, what if you do not have a lot of time to prepare?

Don't worry. As a businessperson, you will never be called upon to discuss issues that you know nothing about. You will usually be called to speak on something that you are familiar with: something related to your job or your industry. Your main problem then, is, how to organize your knowledge or the research you have done in a logical form.

And that is where having some frameworks in mind can be helpful.

In giving support to our opinions, we already learned PREP.

Point

Reason

Example

Point

The above framework can be useful when you have to develop a brief presentation and you need to organize yourself fast. If you choose three points to highlight, then the framework becomes something like what you see on the next page.

Introduction

Point 1:

Reason

Example

Point

Point 2:

Reason

Example

Point

Point 3

Reason

Example

Point

Conclusion

Practice

Prepare a mini-speech with an Introduction that lists three points you want to make. Then, explain each of the three points with reasons, examples, facts and figures, etc., and then end the whole thing with a Conclusion.

You may choose one of the following topics

1. Best way to improve a company's image

2. What is innovation?

3. Cybersecurity

4. Companies should adopt work uniforms.

5. Employees should know one another's salaries.

6. Ways to reduce expenses in a company

7. The importance of ethics in business

8. Business trips: challenges and opportunities

9. Improving harmony in the workplace

10. Intellectual property protection

Introduction
Point 1:
Reason
Example
Point
Point 2:
Reason
Example
Point
Point 3:
Reason
Example
Point
Conclusion

UNIT 21
PPF: Past , Present, Future

The Spanish-American author, George Santayana, is credited with saying that, "Those who cannot remember the past are condemned to repeat it." History has many lessons to teach, and serious students try not to make the same mistakes that others have made in the past.

In business as well, if we are familiar with what has been tried in the past, we can save ourselves a lot of heartache.

Using this framework also allows us to contribute to discussions or to make mini-presentations where we are able to present some information about the past, then pivot to the present, and later reflect on some possibilities for the future.

Let's consider a simple example when someone has asked you to talk about your career.

Past　　　　When I started work in this company ten years ago, we did not have a good enough planning system, so we were often late on projects. I was fortunate to join the company at a time when the leadership was really looking for a solution to that problem. So, I became part of an ambitious planning team that worked day and night to improve our systems.

Present　　　Today, I'm happy that our project planning protocol is one of the best in the world. We are able to go from drawing board to market in record time. We almost always have everything laid out clearly and this allows us to meet our daily, weekly, or monthly commitments.

Future   In the near future, we are going to update our planning system so that we can be even more efficient. What excites me about my career to date is that thanks to our planning system, all employees are able to truly enjoy their work. I'm really proud to have been a part of the changes that have taken place in the company.

There are many occasions, both personal and professional where we can expand our communication by using PPF. Let's practice.

PPF PRACTICE

1. The content of my job: Past, Present, Future

2. Professional relationships I have formed

3. Managers I have known and the kind of manager I should be

4. My experience with technology

5. Customer engagement: Evolution or Revolution?

6. The Skills that will Rule the Future

7. Business travel - experience and future expectations

8. My international travel experience

9. Leadership lessons

10. The use of social networking sites by company employees during working hours

Introduction

Point 1 (Past):

Reason

Example

Point

Point 2 (Present):

Reason

Example

Point

Point 3 (Future):

Reason

Example

Point

Conclusion

UNIT 22
Quick Intro to a Mini-Presentation

Establishing a positive connection with your audience is one of the surest ways to ensure that audience members pay attention to what you have to say. There are a number of ways to establishing a quick connection with your audience. One, of course, is showing that you have something in common with them. Thus, a speaker visiting from another city will often mention the last time he or she was in the city where the speaking is taking place. If the speaker has any good memories about the previous visit, such as the hospitality of the people, or a meeting with some beloved figure in the city, the speaker talks about it and gets a warm applause.

Others prefer to begin with some kind of joke, which can be risky, if for any reason, the audience does not catch on to it.

The safest and most straightforward way to begin a speech, however, may be the following, **Quick Intro,** which has three main parts:

Most people think...

For example,....

I think....

When you are able to make a point that most people agree with, you start on a positive note. This has the potential of making people receptive to your message, and allows you to move on to the main point you want to talk about. But, just making a general statement about what most people think is not enough.

Giving an example, helps to make the point much more concrete. After that, you can say what you really think, along with the points that you want to make in the mini presentation.

Here's an example:

Most people think that we are living in one of the greatest periods of technological boom in history. **For example,** the number of devices that we carry in our bags continues to grow, for example, smartphones, tablets, and gaming consoles. **I think t**hat we should find a way to incorporate these devices into our educational system and I want to explore three points with you.

1) Gaming and communications devices children are most comfortable with
2) Why we learn best what we truly love
3) How we can convert children from users or players to makers or inventors

The Three Points

When we present our three points upfront, we signal to the audience what our roadmap is. This is called signposting, as it gives the audience an idea of where the presentation is going.

Also, don't explain the three points in your introduction. Just mention them. The explanation will come later. Make sure that your three points are short and to the point.

Establishing Authority

Before you launch into your Quick Intro, if you have to introduce yourself, please do so. As you introduce yourself, it may be a good idea to establish your credentials or your experience so that the audience can appreciate why you are the right person to be talking to them at that moment about that partciular subject.

> *Good evening. Thanks for such a wonderful introduction. Let me add that I've been an educator for 25 years and it's a great pleasure for me to be among people like you who show in your daily work such a deep commitment to educating our young ones. I'm sure you'll agree that....*

In the above, the speaker tries to establish authority by disclosing the years of experience and tries to highlight the common ground between the speaker and the audience by pointing out the deep commitment that all of them share.

Putting It All Together

Once you have your Quick Intro, and you know your PREP and your PPF, you are ready to give a presentation even when you do not have a great deal of time to prepare.

Use Points, not Sentences

If you do not have a lot of time to prepare, the worst thing you can do is to start writing your speech in complete sentences. Rather than that, write down the points you want to talk about. As noted earlier, you will most likely be talking about a subject you already know about. So, writing down the points will serve as a trigger for the ideas you want to present. A good idea is to jot down the points you want to cover quickly, and then give yourself some extra time to practice giving the speech using just the points rather than sentences.

IBC: Introduction, Body, & Conclusion

In the English-speaking world, a lot of speeches follow a very definite pattern. There is an introduction, a body, and a conclusion. If you have three points that you want to make, then your body is going to include details about those three points.

Learning from Aristotle: Ethos, Pathos, & Logos

Aristotle, over 2,000 years ago, learned and forged the key to persuasion. We may have the key, but are we willing to open the door?

Ethos

If someone comes to talk to you, and you already believe that the person is a scoundrel, you will probably dismiss whatever the person says. The person's bad character gets in the way of your putting any faith in what he or she has to say. This is what the introduction of a speaker usually does. When a speaker is properly introduced, it helps to establish the credibility of the speaker and makes the audience receptive for the speaker's message. If a speaker is not properly introduced, then, the speaker has to take on that responsibility of sharing with the audience the reason for being on the stage!

Short Notice Speaking Template

On the next page is a template that you can use to prepare a mini-presentation. In such a case, rather than writing long sentences, focus on putting down the key points and then using the points as a basis for your speech.

If you write down complete sentences, it almost forces you to read to the audience, which breaks your connection with them.

On the other hand, if you jot down points, you can use them as triggers or memory joggers and then go on to express from the heart what you want to convey.

Speech Title:

Intro	
Point 1	
Point 2	
Point 3	
Conclusion P P F	

Mini-Speech Practice

Choose a topic below and prepare a brief speech. Be sure to jot down points rather than sentences. Use frameworks such as Quick Intro, PREP, and PPF to speed up the process.

1. Challenges for retailers who move into other countries.

2. First mover versus second mover.

3. Common challenges with mergers and acquisitions.

4. Preparing for a negotiation

5. Products and services you would pay a premium for and why

6. Family-owned businesses

7. Capsule hotels

8. Entrepreneurship

9. How to deal with mistakes in the workplace

10. Use of touch screen terminals at eateries

UNIT 23
Chairperson or Facilitator?

Chair :   the person who is the leader of a meeting, organization, committee, or event

Facilitator :   one that helps to bring about an outcome (as learning, productivity, or communication) by providing indirect or unobtrusive assistance, guidance, or supervision

The word Chairperson (or Chair, Chairman, Chairwoman) is sometimes used in place of Facilitator. A facilitator is someone who acts like a catalyst at a meeting and makes sure that everyone gets heard. In this book, the words are used interchangeably. So, whether you call yourself a chairperson or a facilitator, you are expected to ensure that the meeting achieves the purpose for which it was called.

A good chairperson/facilitator:
- is attentive
- ensures that all voices are heard
- controls the flow of the agenda
- raises questions that others may be ignoring
- challenges the participants to think deeply
- serves as a referee

Discussion

1) Talk about a time you saw someone do a masterful job of running a meeting.

2) Talk about a time when you thought that the facilitator failed.

UNIT 24
When You are the Facilitator/ Chairperson

Being a meeting facilitator or the chairperson is a very important responsibility. Primarily, this means making sure that the purpose for which the meeting was called is achieved whether it is resolving a conflict, coming up with ideas for a proposal, or giving new assignments to staff members.

In almost every group, you are bound to find people who feel comfortable expressing themselves and those who need to be encouraged to express themselves. If you want to benefit from the collective wisdom of those at the meeting, then you have to get everyone to participate.

A good facilitator/chairperson does not use the meeting as an opportunity to focus on himself or herself. To achieve the purpose of the meeting and to avoid groupthink, a facilitator will:

- avoid stating his or her preference at the beginning of the meeting
- urge members to raise objections and concerns
- be willing to consider other viewpoints
- get members to think of alternative scenarios
- encourage everyone to play the role of critical evaluator

Discussion

1) How do you feel when your ideas are criticized during a meeting?

2) What kind of feedback would you welcome from others?

UNIT 25
Meeting Minutes

Record keeping is important for any organization. When you are the chairperson or facilitator, it is important to choose one person to take the minutes.

Meeting minutes are simply the official record of the proceedings at the meeting. Here are a few reasons why meeting minutes are taken: To keep a permanent record of decisions made, actions that ought to be taken, who ought to take the action, and when the decision ought to be implemented.

In fact, in some organizations members rotate in taking on the duty of meeting secretary. In other situations, a designated organization secretary may be responsible for taking the minutes.

The modern world presents many options for how one might record the minutes at a meeting.

BEFORE THE MEETING: CHOOSE YOUR PAD, POD, OR iPAD?
Some people might choose the old-fashioned approach and use a pen and pad. Others might choose a recording device or write on their laptop or tablet computer.

Before you leave for the meeting, double-check to see that you have a pen or pencil, paper or notebook, or an electronic device such as an IPad that is charged. Make sure that you have in full working order the tools you need to do your job as minute taker. It's an important job.

Review Previous Minutes

If the organization has a record of minutes from previous minutes, get some copies and study them. This is because different organizations have their own special ways of doing things, and this includes minute taking.

- What is the preferred method of organizing the minutes?
- How much detail is captured?
- What is the level of formality?
- Is there an existing template that you can follow?

Get a copy of the agenda

An agenda usually includes information that will help you do a better job of taking minutes. It typically includes the following:

- Attendees
- Speakers
- Meeting time/period
- Venue
- Activities
- Chair/facilitator
- Topics for discussion

Before the meeting, let the facilitator send you a copy of the agenda or any materials that will be distributed at the meeting. Your prior familiarity with these items will make your job easier. This also applies to people's names. If you know the names of the other participants ahead of time, then, you don't have to go through the 'pain' of asking people to spell their names.

> *"A person's name is to him or her the sweetest and most important sound in any language."*
>
> - Dale Carnegie

Chat with the Chairperson – Before the Meeting

Find out the level of formality of the meeting. This can make a difference in the kind of minutes you write. It is important to get comfortable with the chairperson so that if you need to clarify something, you will not hold back from doing so. If you are not sure about something and you do not ask and you put down the wrong information, this could be costly for the organization and for you personally. So, be prepared to seek clarification when necessary.

Be an Early Bird

The worst thing you can do as a minute taker is to attend the meeting late. Go early, and make sure that you have the tools you need. If you are using electronic equipment, make sure that they are in good shape, charged, or with access to an electrical source.

The most basic items are a pen and paper, but some like to have on hand such items as a highlighter or colored pens and a notepad. Having extra writing instruments on hand can be very helpful.

Get to Know About the Meeting Participants

If you are at the kind of meeting where everyone has a name tag, then your job is going to be easier.

Thus, if it is possible for you to make such an arrangement, do so. If not, get a copy of the agenda ahead of time and familiarize yourself with the names of attendees. Also, if you go to the meeting early, you can get to meet some of these attendees before the meeting starts. Having such a meeting will help you remember names and aid in your task of writing down who said what at the meeting.

WHAT TO DO DURING THE MEETING

- Pay attention when people are introducing themselves and write down the names of those that you didn't know before.

- Knowing who is who is critical because you will need to record who makes what point, in particular, the major points at the meeting.

- Write down the time the meeting starts.

- You will also later write down what time the meeting is adjourned or ended.

- It may be overwhelming at a meeting where ideas are flying around rapidly. Keep calm and record only the main points, not every word that is said.

- Include any items that are mentioned for discussion in the future.

WHAT TO DO AFTER THE MEETING

- Following the meeting, type the minutes, including the list of names of those who attended

- Have the name of the organization or club at the top of the sheet and indicate what the purpose of the meeting was

- Include your name at the bottom after words such as the following: SUBMITTED BY ....

- Submit the minutes of the meeting to the facilitator or chairperson of the meeting or whoever is designated as being responsible for it.

MEETING MINUTES TEMPLATE

These days you can find free templates online for many routine office reports. This includes meeting minutes. If your organization has a standard meeting minutes template, make sure you get your hands on it. If not, you can find a suitable template free online or create your own. A sample template is presented below:

XYZ ORGANIZATION - Globalization Committee

Subject:

Date: Time: Location:

Meeting Chairman:

Attendees:

Absent:

Meeting / Discussion:

_____

_____

_____

_____

Action Items:	Assigned to:	Date Due:	Notes

Future Meetings: **Date:**   **Time:**   **Place:**

SUBMITTED BY: _____

Practice

Hold meetings using the topics as a theme. For each meeting, have one person serve as a facilitator, another as a timekeeper, and yet another as a minutetaker.

1. Making private phone calls during work time

2. Marketing in the 21st century

3. Leadership development

4. Company branding

5. Product positioning

6. Changing customer needs

7. Price competition

8. Customer relationships

9. Localization issues for multinational companies

10. Brand loyalty

UNIT 26
Ground Rules

Setting a few ground rules before a meeting starts can help make participation in a meeting comfortable for everyone. This is particularly the case if the meeting involves a large number of people. You may include the ground rules with the agenda if you are ab;e to send these out befre the meeting. in most cases, however, the agenda is given out at the meeting. Be sure to remind atendees of these ground rules.

You might let attendees know, for example, that an individual who wants to speak should raise his or her hand. Try to figure out which ground rules would most apply to your particular meeting.

Here are some common ground rules:

• be punctual	• focus on issues, not personalities
• start on time	• take notes
• end on time	• treat everyone with respect
• put smart phones on vibrate	• be constructive
• participate actively	• ask relevant questions
• no unnecessary interruptions	• wait for acknowledgment from chairperson before speaking
• be brief and to the point	• only one speaker at a time
• come prepared	• focus on the topic under discussion

Discussion
What other ground rules do you think could help make a meeting run more smoothly?

UNIT 27
Getting the Ball Rolling

If the meeting is expected to start at 1:00 p.m., don't wait until that time before getting everyone to settle down. A few minutes before the appointed time, sound the gavel, and tell participants to be ready for the meeting to start. This will alert people who are chatting or roaming aimlessly around to begin to focus on the impending meeting. If done well, by the time the meeting time strikes, everyone will be in his or her seat ready for the facilitator to begin the proceedings.

The meeting may begin with the chairperson calling everyone's attention and welcoming participants to the meeting.

If you are the chair of the meeting you want people to feel relaxed. A few appropriate words of welcome will usually set the mood. For example,

> *Shall we start?*
> *Please be seated, everyone.*
>
> *First of all, let me say thanks to all of you for taking the time to attend this meeting. This is a crucial meeting for our organization and we are happy that we can have the chance to hear what you all have to say about the upcoming changes.*

Welcoming Participants

There are a number of phrases that the facilitator can use to get the meeting started. Here are a few of them:

• Shall we start?	• Hello everyone. I'm really you could all make it.
• Let's get the ball rolling.	• We've got a lot to cover so the sooner we begin the better.
• Welcome everyone.	• I'm really grateful you could all attend because we have some serious business to discuss.
• It seems everyone is here, so let's get started.	

Practice

Choose one of the phrases that you're most comfortable with. Say it as naturally as possible.

Introductions: Facilitator and Attendees

If it's an internal meeting, quite likely, everyone knows the facilitator. But if there is any chance that some of the participants do not know one another, it might be a good idea to get the introductions out of the way, so that everyone will know who they are dealing with.

In particular, if there are some guests that have come to the meeting because of their special expertise or because they have been invited to play an importnat role at the meeting, it is important to give them the proper respect by giving them a glowing introduction. This will also make the visitor feel comfortable and at home and perhaps make it easier for him or her to contribute.

Be sure not to overlook anyone. If you want people to stand and introduce themselves, please say so. If you want them to introduce themselves while sitting, please say so. Don't let someone start introducing himself while sitting and then ask the person to stand up! Be careful not to bring up information that people might consider too personal, for example, "Bob is on his third marrriage. He's pretty wild, isn't he? Ha ha haa!!!"

That would be a no-no.

Among the key pieces of information people might volunteer in their introductions are the following:

- First and last name
- Company name / division / department
- Title or role / reason for attending the meeting
- Location / branch office

Some facilitators prefer to begin with the purpose of the meeting before getting to the introductions. Others prefer to get the introductions out of the way before getting to the reason for the meeting. As the facilitator, you have to decide which is preferable for you.

Useful phrases for making introductions
- Let me begin by introducing myself...
- I would like to introduce...
- It is a pleasure for me to introduce our new HR manager...
- You might have noticed that we have a few new faces here...
- I'd like everyone to say a few words about their backround...

Practice
Choose one of the phrases above and practice saying it as naturally as possible.

Roll Call (Apologies / Non-attendance)

Before a meeting, there is usually an expectation about who is going to attend the meeting. In many cases, the names of expected attendees will be on the agenda.

So, after the introductions, the facilitator might want to do a formal roll call to acknowledge those who were able to attend and those who were not able to attend.

Usually, in this case, the attention is more on those who were unable to attend. Quite often, the person who could not attend might have already spoken to the facilitator or chairperson or the secretary. If that is the case, the news will be shared as to who could not attend, and possibly the reason, if appropriate to do so.

Useful phrases for doing the roll call/apologies
- How wonderful that we have full attendance at this meeting today...
- Ms. Sanay is on vacation, so she couldn't be here.
- We are fortunate to have Mr. Willoughby here today. He is going to do us the honor of taking the minutes for the meeting.
- James is here in place of Laura, who is currently on a business trip

Model
A couple of staff members were not able to make it. These are John Preston and Chieko Yamamura. We'll catch up with them later.

Practice
Choose one of the phrases above and say it as naturally as possible. You could add some names to make it sound realistic.

Objective of the Meeting

Hopefully, all the participants have in front of them a copy of the agenda. Quite often the objective of the meeting is written on the agenda. The facilitator can announce this as a way to refocus the attention of participants.

- Please note that our meeting today is going to focus on...
- The purpose of our meeting today is...
- The objective of this meeting is...
- In case anyone is still wondering about the purpose for this meeting, it is...

Practice

Choose an objective and use one of the above phrases to introduce it. Let it sound as natural as possible.

Agenda

While it is important for everyone to come to a meeting fully prepared, there are occasions where some participants might not have had the chance to do the necessary preparatory work. So, going over the agenda is usually a good idea. Here is an example:

Today, there are five items on the agenda. I am not sure if we can get through all of them, but if you keep your comments short and to the point, maybe we can. As you can see on the agenda, first, we are going to hear from the VP R&D, who will update us on the progress of key projects in her department. Then, we will hear from our four department heads. After that, we will discuss the problems facing the purchasing department. I hope you have some ideas about how we can resolve those issues. Next will be the issue about how many people we should have on hand during the holidays. Finally, we will get an update about the holiday party and how we can make it memorable for stafff.

Agenda

2:30 pm	Meeting starts
	Welcome and introductions
2:35 pm	Key Projects update (VP R&D
2:45 pm	Department Heads
3:00 pm	Purchasing Department Issues
3:20 pm	Skeleton staff (holidays)
3:25 pm	Holiday party
3:30 pm	Close

Ground Rules

Some people never pay attention at meetings. Worse, they begin to chat with others while the meeting is going on. Some also make it a point not to say anything at all. If you want the meeting to be productive, you have to consider what the most worrisome potential issues are and present ground rules to cover them.

For some facilitators, the problem they are confronted with is how to tell a meeting participant to stop saying the same thing over and over again while others wait for the chance to speak. In other cases, the problem might be a person who is fixated on his mobile phone all the time the meeting is going on.

Here is how a facilitator might set some ground rules.

> Your time is important, so I hope we can cooperate to make this meeting a productive one. To achieve this, let's set a few ground rules. I hope everyone tries very hard to abide by them. There are only four of them.
>
> *One, let's stick to the agenda. If you have any topics that are off this agenda, let's discuss them at another time. Two, please don't interrupt others. I want everyone to have his or her say.*
> *Three, if you want to speak, please raise your hand and wait for the chairperson/facilitator (of course, that's me) to acknowledge you. And four, please put your smartphones on vibrate. Can we all live by this?*

or

> *We need to hear from everybody. This is the only way we can set the proper direction for this department. If you have something to say, just raise your hand slightly, and I will call on you. Now, let's take a look at the first item on the agenda, which is...*

MINUTES OF THE LAST MEETING

Minutes are brief notes about discussions and decisions made at a meeting. If your meeting is one that is routine and is a continuation of a previous meeting, then it is likely that one of the first items on the agenda will be th reading of the minutes of the last meeting.

This will help update all present about some of the discussions the group had in the past and to continue with any items that were not concluded at the previous meeting.

Practice
Think of one or two ground rules you will set for a meeting. Practice what you will say about ground rules to get everyone on the same page.

_____

_____

_____

_____

_____

_____

_____

UNIT 28
WIRO-AG Practice

When you are the facilitator, you have a pretty important responsibility. If you don't manage the meeting well, it can easily go off the rails. So, you have to be vigilant from start to finish.

a)   Let's say, you are the facilitator at the next meeting of your department. Prepare an **Agenda** with three items and a **Purpose/Objective** for the meeting.

b)   Prepare your welcome and introduction to the meeting using the following *aide-memoire* (memory aid).

Welcome:	**W**
Introductions:	**I**
Roll Call / Apologies:	**R**
Objective:	**O**
Agenda:	**A**
Ground Rules:	**G**

Please make sure you remember the above sequence.

Model:

Welcome:

> Hello, welcome to the first meeting of the second quarter. I hope everyone is doing well.

Introductions:

> For the benefit of the new ones among us, let me introduce myself. I'm the acting head of the marketing department, and I'll be in this role until at least the end of the year. Okay, can I get everyone to say a few words of introduction. If you can give your name, your department, and how long you've been with the company, that would be great.

Roll Call / Apologies:

> Thanks for the introductions. Sally and Waymo, we're very happy to have you in our corner. Now, I got a message from two people, Edna Vanderpuy and Lorna Akasaka that they are on an emergeny business trip. So, we'll catch up with them when they return.

Objective:

> Anyway, today the main thing we're going to talk about is how we can improve our customer service. We've been getting some unbelievable complaints in recent weeks, and we need to do something about them fast.

Agenda:

> One of the papers in front of you is the agenda. Please take a look at it. As you can see, we're going to touch on three areas:
>
>> 1) Recent complaints from customers
>> 2) Our response time
>> 3) The quality of our solutions

Ground Rules:

> In order to make sure that the meeting runs well so we can get out of here within an hour, let's agree on some ground rules. a) Please keep your comments brief, b) Don't interrupt others, and c) don't hold back your ideas

Practice (Use the topics below or participants' own topics)

Each person will have an opportunity to serve as a facilitator and to welcome participants by going through the WIRO-AG process from beginning to end. Take some time to think of some agenda items that will fit in with the objectives of the meeting that you decide on.

1. Monitoring performance

2. Regulation and compliance

3. Data management

4. Budget control

5. Talent recruitment

6. Customer service

7. Managing company reputation

8. Dealing with change

9. Cybercrime

10. Reducing energy use

UNIT 29
Introducing a Fresh Topic

A meeting, by definition, involves an exchange of ideas between two or more people. It is a gathering of people for the purpose of exchanging views and coming to some satisfactory conclusion. A meeting is not a one-person show! If the chairperson is not careful, he or she might spend a lot of time talking on and on and on. The other members might just sit there and hope that they are given the chance to share their views. To avoid rambling, use the following 5-step process to introduce a new topic for discussion. This could be individual items on the agenda.

AI-BRQ

Attention	Draw the attention of the participants.
Issue	Mention the ISSUE or TOPIC you want discussed.
Background	Give some details about the issue, for example, how the issue became important. This will help those who have not had the chance to prepare to appreciate the scope of the discussion and what is at stake.
Relevance	Establish the connection between the issue and the meeting participants. How are they affected by the issue? Why is it necessary for them to be involved?
Question	End with a question...pause for a moment... and invite someone[1] at the meeting to respond.

---

1 Be careful who you call. If you have been paying attention to the attendees, their body language will help you determine who is ready to speak and who might not be quite ready yet.

The meeting facilitator should come prepared to introduce the key issues for discussion. If the matter is not clear in the mind of the facilitator, it is going to be difficult for participants to understand. Smart facilitators will come prepared. This might mean practicing beforehand just how they are going to introduce the topic at hand.

Here are some useful phrases for introducing an issue or topic.

- I would like to start by...
- First of all, I'd like to note that..
- The main issue for which we have called this meeting is...
- The principal issue, it seems to me, is...
- I'd like to open the meeting with some remarks about....
-
- We are going to focus on...
- The main problem is...
- The main issue for us to consider is..
- I'd like us to focus on the issue of...
- The question of...is one we need to consider seriously.
-
- I'd like to highlight....
- The most significant element for us is...
- To start with, let's consider...
- Let's begin by considering...
- The main reason for this meeting is...

Model: **You are the discussion leader. Using the 5-Step Method (AI-BRQ: Attention, Issue, Background, Relevance, Question), open a meeting on the following topics. Several models have been provided for you below.**

Model (AI-BRQ)
(New Media Marketing Strategy)

Attention: Now that we've finished with introductions, let's begin the meeting, shall we?

Issue: As you can see from the agenda, we are going to begin our discussion on the topic of new media and how our company can leverage some of the new tools and platforms available.

Background: I'm sure you will all agree that the growth of new media has been spectacular. It's hard to keep up with new platforms popping up every few months. There is Facebook, Twitter, LinkedIn, Buzzfeed, and so many networking sites, all promising wonders for our business. It's a bit confusing but we cannot wait forever to make use of these platforms. At the same time, we don't want to plunge into the new media space and waste money or make unnecessary mistakes.

Relevance: At the moment, our sales numbers are holding steady but we cannot afford to stand still. We need to be growing and if we do not take advantage of the new media, we are going to begin to slide back. Certainly, none of us wants that.

Question: Satoshi-san, you are quite knowledgeable about what is going on in the social networking sites. When you look at our business right now, ***where would you suggest we take our first few steps?***

Model: Initiating a Discussion

1. Customer service
Attention:

Welcome everyone. I'm pretty happy that everyone was able to make it. Make yourselves comfortable. This meeting will run about two hours, so after about an hour or so, we'll take a ten-minute break. If you have something to say, please raise your hand and I'll acknowledge you. I'm sure you're all ready to participate actively.

Issue:

The main reason we are meeting today is the issue of CUSTOMER SERVICE.

Background:

For many years, one of the cornerstones of our success was our exceptional customer service. We used to get a lot of comments from clients about our incredible attention to detail. These were not idle comments made to make us feel good. Customers followed their comments with fresh order and repeat business.

Relevance:

In the last few months, it looks like we've been getting more complaints than praise and more requests for refunds than repeat business. Clearly, we have all slipped somewhere and I hope that by putting our heads together,we can come up with some strategies that will help us regain the trust of our clients.

Question:

Ms. Kinjo, how do you feel about the flood of complaints we are getting these days?

Model: Initiating a Discussion

2. Information sharing within a company

Attention:

Shall we begin? Thanks very much for coming. We have a lot to talk about and I am sure you're all eager to contribute to the meeting.

Issue:

I want us to begin with the issue of information sharing within the company.

Background:

I'm sure you will all agree that we have a lot of talent within the company and many of you have proven that you are some of the most incredible problem solvers anywhere. Still, there have been times when projects have slowed down because someone lacked some key information that could drive the project forward. I know there is a lot of informal sharing of information going on but this has not always helped when the person that could most benefit from a certain piece of information is outside the loop and thus cannot do what he or she needs to do.

Relevance:

When the right people fail to have the right piece of information at the right time, the result can be needless delays, which impacts upon our ability to complete projects which in turn translates into a weak bottom line...and lower bonuses...I hope the word "bonus" gets your attention (LAUGHTER)...

Question:

Let me start with you, Team Leader Kanako Ishikawa. Can you share with us some of the difficulties you have had getting information from some departments?

Practice: Initiating a Discussion

3. Exporting products and services

Attention:
Issue:
Background:
Relevance:
Question:

Practice: Initiating a Discussion

4. New computer systems

Attention:
Issue:
Background:
Relevance:
Question:

Practice: Initiating a Discussion

5. Work-life balance

Attention:

Issue:

Background:

Relevance:

Question:

Practice: Initiating a Discussion

6. Employee turnover

Attention:

Issue:

Background:

Relevance:

Question:

PRACTICE: Initiating a Discussion (WITHOUT NOTES)

Practice introducing the following topics without writing down any notes. In other words, try to craft your Attention, Issue, Background, Relevance, and Question off the top of your head. This will make your introduction much more natural and in line with what participants at a meeting will expect.

1. Competition

2. Using social media for business promotion

3. Protecting intellectual property

4. Compliance with government regulations

5. Increasing cost of supplies

6. Finding qualified employees

7. Unusually long breaks by employees

8. Office cleanliness

9. Cost-effective advertising

10. Employee training

UNIT 30
Discussion Leader
(Chairperson/Facilitator): POINTS TO PONDER

While it is clear that it is challenging being a facilitator, with preparation, you can certainly do it well and even excel at it. You can make your life a lot easier if you review and stick with some of the suggestions below:

ENGAGE...BUT DON'T EMBARRASS ANYONE

If you are the chairperson you want to get the most out of the meeting. This may mean ensuring that everyone participates actively. If you are alert to the body language of those present at the meeting, however, you will be able to pick up clues about who may be eager to speak and who may be reluctant to speak.

QUICK VERSUS SLOW STARTERS

Some people are able to jump into a discussion very quickly without a lot of preparation.

Others need to hear more discussion before they can gather the courage to participate.

If you are the chairperson and you call someone who is not quite prepared to participate, you might embarrass the person.

This may temporarily affect the mood in the meeting room. So, you need to be alert and watch for signs.

A person who is trying to be inconspicuous may just not be ready to contribute. There are also some individuals who talk too much without contributing anything significant to the discussion. A smart chairperson will encourage participation from a broader spectrum of people rather than have one person dominate the discussion.

There are also those who may pretend to hide while in fact seeking to be called! As a chairperson, you have to be fully alert if you are going to be able to decode the behavior of meeting attendees well. Whatever you do, be considerate of the attendees. Try not to embarrass anyone. Encourage people to share their feelings and make people feel happy that they shared their thoughts. When participants feel valued, they are much more likely to want to share. Creating an atmosphere of respect is therefore essential.

- Choose someone to be a timekeeper
- Choose someone to be a minute taker
- Be prepared (do some research - includes talking to key figures)
- Have a list of questions prepared
- Raise new questions as the discussion moves along

- Probe for details
- Ask for clarification
- Ensure that quiet members have an opportunity to participate
- Be prepared to politely wind down anyone who rambles
- Keep track of time

Discussion
Which of the above will be easiest for you to do and which will be challenging for you to do. Why?

More points to ponder

- Ask for a vote on an issue if this is the way things are done in your organization
- Record the results of the vote or have them recorded for you.
- Keep track of all action items.
- Keep track of who is responsible for what.
- Make sure that minutes are read at the end of the meetng and that they accurately reflect what was discussed.
- Summarise the discussion

Discussion

Which of the above will be easiest for you to do and which will be challenging for you to do. Why?

Practice
One person will serve as a facilitator. Try to have a discussion that goes two or three rounds. This would mean asking one another questions, and advancing the discussion so that it gets deeper.

1. Localization issues for multinational companies

2. The ecofriendly workplace

3. Workplace bullying

4. Motivating employees

5. Privacy in the workplace

6. The company cafeteria

7. Bringing children to the workplace

8. Breaking cultural barriers

9. Marketing through online videos

10. Internal negotiations

UNIT 31
MMM:
Masterful Meeting Management

There are so many elements you have to keep in mind if you want to be successful running your meeting. Let's review them a little more.

Attendance:

Make sure attendees understand their role at the meeting.

Agenda:

Attendees ought to have received a copy of their agenda ahead of time (e.g., one week)

Changes to Agenda:

When those invited to the meeting see an error on the agenda, they should inform the person responsible for the agenda immediately. Also, if the person slated to preside over the meeting has new items or changes he or she wishes to make, such changes should be sent as quickly as possible or a new agenda should be issued.

Preparation:

Participants who have special roles should ensure that they are well prepared by the date and time of the meeting.

Break:

For a meeting that runs for two hours or more, it is the course of wisdom to build in a five-to-ten-minute break.

Acknowledgment:

Participants can contribute to an orderly meeting by raising their hand slightly to get the attention of the chairperson when they have something to say.

Interruptions:

Unnecessary interruptions slow down a meeting and can be a source of resentment for those who are repeatedly interrupted. There are occasions, however, when an immediate interruption is necessary. When someone has made an important error and does not self-correct, interrupting to draw the person's attention to the error is all right.

Bringing Another in to Respond to a Question

The facilitator should be especially alert to ensure that everyone participates actively. If the facilitator finds that someone has the expertise to answer a question but that the person is holding back, it would only be fair to give that person the opportunity by directly calling on him or her.

- I wonder if Ms XXX would like to respond to that...
- If I may, I'd like to ask Mr YYY to answer that...
- I believe that the best person to handle that question is...
- Perhaps, XXXX would care to answer that...
- I think Ms X is more qualified an I am to respond.

Bringing Another in to Make a Point

- I suppose Ms XXXX would like to makea point...
- I would like to ask Mr XXX to share his views on this matter...
- Allow me to give the floor to Mr...
- Ms. XXX, I believe you have something to say here...

Seeking Understanding

The facilitator would also want to check continually to ensure that the whole team is on the same page. In fact, this might be the responsibility of only the facilitator. Every participant can check with others to be sure that others are following one's argument.

- Do we all agree on that?
- Do you follow my point?
- Are you with me so far?

Summarizing Your Argument (Can be used by facilitator/participants)

- Finally, I would like to say...
- Summing up the discussion...
- In short...
- To sum up...
- My final point is...
- To put everything in a nutshell...
- To put the whole manner in a nutshell...
- The gist of the issue is that...

UNIT 32
Summarizing the Meeting

As the Chairperson or Facilitator, after going through the discussions, you would want to summarize the discussion. This would include all the main points made, including some of the disagreements.

Perhaps, throughout the discussion, three different ideas emerged. Mentioning these ideas in a summary will allow everyone to be reminded of what has been discussed.

The overall summary is also an opportunity to correct any misperceptions. If the Chairperson makes an error in the summary, one or more of the members might jump in and correct him or her.

What happens after the summary by the Chairperson depends on the goal of the meeting. It may be that some individuals at the meeting will be assigned to follow through on some items. If so, the secretary/minute taker would record both the item in question and the individuals assigned to them.

Useful phrases for summarizing a discussion/meeting
- Okay, now let me summarize what we covered today...
- The first thing we discussed was...and we decided to....
- Another point we covered was...for which we came to the conclusion that...
- Finally, we talked about...and the whole group decided that...

- Did I miss anything?

Practice

Participants can take turns serving as facilitators. When serving as a facilitator, be sure to choose a timekeeper and a minute taker. Also, practice going through the whole process from WIRO-AG through AI-BRQ and finally a summary.

1. Difficult conversations in the workplace

2. Making yourself indispensable on the job

3. Building business networks

4. Protecting a company's public image

5. Personal goals versus company goals

6. Effective mentorship

7. Cloud computing

8. Protecting customer data

9. Corporate training systems

10. Working abroad

UNIT 33
Coming to a Decision

Different organizations have different ways of coming to a decision. This may depend on the culture within which you are operating. Or, it may be because your organization has adopted a particular stance towards decisionmaking. Here are some common ways of coming to a decision following a meeting.

Autocratic

In some organizations, after all the discussions are over, the leader simply decides what to do. Everyone simply follows whatever the leader decides to do. In fact, some leaders may not even inform those present at the meeting what they intend to do. This kind of decision-making may be very fast. It may also mean that nothing gets done until the boss takes a stand.

Consensus

The consensus form of decision-making, however, values both the opinions of those in the majority and those in the minority. In this case, the leader becomes just one of the individuals involved in coming to an agreement. Mutual respect is required for consensus decision-making to work and it can be quite slow as well since some individuals may require more time to buy into the ideas being considered.

Democratic

Democratic rule, unlike the consensus form of decision-making, simply requires that a majority of those present agree on a particular position. Whereas the views of the minority may have been listened to during the discussion, once the majority decide to go with a position, that becomes the official position.

Practice

Participants can take turns serving as facilitators. When serving as a facilitator, be sure to choose a timekeeper and a minute taker. Also, practice going through the whole process from WIRO-AG through AI-BRQ and finally a summary. This time, choose one of the decision making methods discussed above and incorporate it into your proceedings.

1. Dealing with business loss

2. The impact of trade wars

3. Electric cars

4. Workplace pranks

5. The plastic waste problem

6. Preparing for natural disasters

7. Paid family leave

8. Retirement activities

9. Patent protection

10. Phishing

UNIT 34
Voting after a Business Discussion

The normal parliamentary procedures for voting are quite complex and few businesses care to follow the strict rules involved. With parliamentary procedures, an item comes up for discussion when one of those at the meeting "makes a motion," that is, formally presents the idea for discussion.In making a motion, the words to use are the following: "I move that..."

In order for the motion or the item to be accepted for discussion, another member has to second the motion. If the amendment is accepted, it will affect the original motion and the wording will be changed to reflect the amendment. Once a motion is seconded, the chairperson opens it up for discussion. In the process of the discussion, some member might suggest an amendment to the original motion, which would mean that some words or some aspect of the motion should be changed.

Model:

Participant A: I move that we take this Friday off because a few people in the office have got the flu.

Participant B: I second the motion.

Facilitator: It has been moved and seconded that "we take this Friday off because a few people in the offie have got the flu." Are you ready to discuss this motion?

Participant C: Madame Facilitator, I would like to make an amendment to the motion.

Facilitator: State your amendment.

After an amendment has been accepted and the original motion has been changed, the chairperson will ask for discussion on the amendment and then take a vote on it. If the amendment fails, the original motion will stand. The use of Robert's Rules of Order can be quite complicated. Parliamentary procedures, using Robert's Rules of Order, come in a huge volume and is popular among groups such as Toastmasters. A meeting that uses Robert's Rules of Order leaves many people perplexed and perhaps unable to participate effectively. For most business meetings, a much simpler approach might work. For one thing, the item that is up for discussion at the meeting may have been on an agenda rather than presented as a special motion. After the discussion, the chairperson might put the question up for a simple vote. For example,

We have been discussing the choice of date for the Christmas party. It seems that quite a number of people favor December 22. Let's put that to a vote.

All those in favor, raise your hand.

> (The Chairperson or another person counts the number of hands raised)

Then, the Chairpersons says,

All those against, raise your hand.

> (The Chairperson or another person counts the number of hands raised).

If more people raised their hand in support of the item, the Chairperson says:

> *The motion has been carried.* The Christmas party will be held on December 22.

Practice

Participants can take turns serving as facilitators. When serving as a facilitator, be sure to choose a timekeeper and a minute taker. Also, practice going through the whole process from WIRO-AG through AI-BRQ and finally a summary. This time, choose one of the decision making methods discussed above and incorporate it into your proceedings.

1. Employee recognition

2. Government regulations

3. Risks companies face

4. Pace of technological change

5. The stars in the organization

6. Team brand

7. The company credit card

8. Employee health

9. Preparing new recruits for success

10. Asking for advice

UNIT 35
Assert Yourself

Going to a meeting with a heart full of fear will not make you very useful there. To ensure that your ideas get into the mix, you need to be assertive. If you want to feel more comfortable at a meeting, especially one that involves people you do not know well, here are a couple of points to keep in mind.

Tips on Being an Assertive Speaker

• **Prepare**

According to the late American author, lecturer, and trainer Dale Carnegie, "Only the prepared speaker deserves to be confident."

• **Mind Your Body Language**

Harvard Business School Professor Amy Cuddy of TEDTalk fame, has said: "When our body language is confident and open, other people respond in kind, unconsciously reinforcing not only their perception of us but also our perception of ourselves."

And Professor Albert Mehrabian of UCLA, has said,,

"Indeed, in the realm of feelings, our facial and vocal expressions, postures, movements, and gestures are so important that when our words contradict the messages contained within them, others mistrust what we say – they rely almost completely on what we do."

• **Speak UP**

Speaking in a very low tone often signals lack of confidence. Remember that you are at the meeting because someone believes in your ability and your potential to contribute. Use that as a source of energy.

- **Ask Questions**

Even if you don't have any points of your own, asking some relevant questions can help move the discussion forward. That can be a worthwhile contribution to the meeting.

- **Jump In**

Some meetings are very orderly. The facilitator has ground rules that ensure that anyone who wants to speak gets a turn. However, there are times when you must have the courage to make your voice heard.

This is particularly the case where there are many people and there is an endless stream of ideas. As soon as someone finishes speaking, or sometimes before one person has completed what she wants to say, another has begun taking the conversation in a new direction. Meanwhile, your turn never comes...

In such a case, work on your timing, so that you can jump in at the right time....

Get to know the participants before the meeting starts

When you are at a meeting where you do not know the participants, it can be intimidating at first. One strategy is to get to the meeting early. Chat with others who will be attending the meeting. Get to know a few people. They will then no longer be strangers, and you will feel more comfortable expressing yourself.

Don't Rush

Harvard Business School Professor Amy Cuddy said in her powerful TED Talk that, "Powerful people initiate speech more often, talk more overall, and make more eye contact while they're speaking than powerless people do. When we feel powerful, we speak more slowly and take more time. We don't rush. We're not afraid to pause. We feel entitled to the time we're using."

Feeling strong?

Practice

Participants can take turns serving as facilitators. When serving as a facilitator, be sure to choose a timekeeper and a minute taker. Also, practice going through the whole process from WIRO-AG through AI-BRQ and finally a summary. This time, choose one of the decision making methods discussed above and incorporate it into your proceedings.

1. Cross-Silo leadership

2. The Problem of Overconfidence

3. Artificial Intelligence

4. Visionary leadership

5. Inclusive leadership

6. The importance of product packaging

7. Public relations: Of what worth?

8. Conspicuous consumption

9. Problem solving in the workplace

10. Doing things right versus doing the right things

UNIT 36
If You Must Interrupt

Ｔhere are occasions when you really must interrupt someone. But, it is important to do so politely. If you rudely interrupt another person, you can easily raise tensions, creating an atmosphere that does not help advance discussion.

You may interrupt when what you have to say is urgent, for example, someone has said something that you need to correct immediately.

Or you may interrupt when someone has said something that is unclear.

A GOOD TIME TO INTERRUPT IS WHEN...
- the other person has just finished talking
- the other person slows down
- the other person pauses
- the other person has spoken long enough
- the speaker seems momentarily confused

Here below are some situations in which it is all right to interrupt:

1) When a speaker is breaking an important rule
2) When a speaker is being impolite to others
3) When you need to add an important point to what has been said

In general, it is not good form to interrupt others, so you need to make sure that you have a good reason. B

Here are a few phrases you might use:

1) Can I just say something here?	8) I hate to cut in like this, but...
2) Pardon me for interrupting, but....	9) Before you move on, I'd like to say something.
3) Let me interject for a moment.	10) Sorry for interrupting, but...
4) Just a moment. I think that....	11) Can I just mention something?
5) May I come in here...	12) Wait a minute...
6) Can I make a point here...	13) Hold on...
7) May I interrupt for a moment...	14) Excuse me for interrupting...

PRACTICE: Pair work

Participant A will read a set of instructions at a normal rate of speech. In order for Participant B to accurately follow the instructions, it might be necessary for Participant B to interrupt. Use appropriate phrases to preface questions. Switch.

Participant A:

Please take out a blank piece of paper. On the blank piece of paper, draw a circle at the top right corner. Draw a rectangle at the top left corner. Draw a star at the bottom left and leave the bottom right blank for now. Write the name of your favorite movie in the middle of the page. Circle the name of your favorite movie. Around the circle, draw four arrows north, south, east, and west of the circle, with the arrows pointing away from the circle. At the tip of each arrow, write down a random two-digit number. Then, write your own first name at the bottom right of the sheet.

Switch. This time, Participant B reads the instructions and Participant A executives them.

Participant B:

Take a piece of paper. Fold it in half so that the length remains the same but the width is half what it was before. Draw a vertical line in the middle, from top to bottom. Then draw a horizontal line in the middle from one side to the next.

At the top left quadrant, write the name of your hometown. At the top right quandrant, write the name of your favorite food. At the bottom left quadrant, draw three circles that touch each other. In each of the circles, write a random three-digit number. After that, turn the paper over. Draw a large circle. In the circle, draw a large square. In the square, draw a triangle. Then, in the triangle, write your first name.

Practice

Participants can take turns serving as facilitators. When serving as a facilitator, be sure to choose a timekeeper and a minute taker. Also, practice going through the whole process from WIRO-AG through AI-BRQ and finally a summary. This time, choose one of the decision making methods discussed above and incorporate it into your proceedings.

1. Custom-made products

2. Division of labor

3. Industry dinosaurs: How not to become one

4. Overconfidence

5. Desperate times call for desperate measures

6. Quality control

7. Disruptive products

8. If it ain't broke, don't fix it: True or false?

9. Cost of advertising

10. Increasing employee satisfaction

UNIT 37
Avoiding Groupthink

If you say something stupid and no one disagrees, then you know you're the boss.
> **- J. Paul Getty, American billionaire**

Groupthink, a term coined by social psychologist Irving Janis in 1972, refers to the situation when members of a group try so hard to be in harmony, that they so easily accept what others say, especially, what the leader says. When this happens, it is possible to make a decision that is wrong -- very wrong!

At a meeting, if the chairperson, who is also the boss, announces that he or she has decided to do something, it is difficult for participants to challenge that decision even when it is very clear that the boss is making a mistake. If a leader does not want such an outcome, it is better for the leader not to indicate what he or she prefers. That way, participants can more honestly express their viewpoints, along with supporting facts or evidence.

No one can possibly achieve any real and lasting success or 'get rich' in business by being a conformist.
> **- J. Paul Getty, American billionaire**

Groupthink can happen if group members:

- consider only a few alternatives
- avoid constructive criticism of one another's ideas
- fail to consider promising options
- do not take into account expert opinion or research
- focus on only a few sources for their data

Practice

Participants can take turns serving as facilitators. When serving as a facilitator, be sure to choose a timekeeper and a minute taker. Also, practice going through the whole process from WIRO-AG through AI-BRQ and finally a summary. This time, choose one of the decision making methods discussed above and incorporate it into your proceedings.

1. Maintenance of equipment

2. Fear of change

3. Raw materials

4. Ways to build trust in the workplace

5. Product recalls

6. JIT - Just In Time system

7. Pareto principle: 20% of problems are serious while 80% are trivial

8. Being in denial

9. Crowdfunding

10. Partnerships for success

UNIT 38
Raising Questions

Both the Chairperson/Facilitator and the meeting participants have to be comfortable with asking questions or being questioned. These questions can help the group to dig deeper and explore widely as they seek to come to a decision.

It is important, therefore, to consider two common types of questions: Open-ended questions and close-ended questions.

Open-ended versus Close-ended questions

When you set up a meeting, part of your goal may be to give out information. In some cases, you want attendees to discuss an issue so that the best ideas will bubble up and help the organization to chart a successful course going forward.

If indeed, you want attendees to express themselves and share their thoughts, then you should avoid asking closed-ended questions.

Close-ended questions

When you ask a close-ended question, it can be answered with a simple YES or NO.

Here are some examples of close-ended questions:
- Have you been to Europe before?
- Have you written the report?
- Do you want to go home early today?
- Do you like surfing the Internet?
- Is the boss in the office?
- Has the secretary come in today?

Think of 3 close-ended questions and write them below:

1. _____

   _____

2. _____

   _____

3. _____

   _____

Open-ended questions

As important as close-ended questions are, they are not very useful in helping you to know the full range of someone's ideas or thoughts on a subject. Open-ended questions allow the person responding to the question to go beyond a one-word answer and to share an opinion, lay out a series of ideas, analyze a situation or draw contrasts. In short, an open-ended question is more likely to yield a richer palette of ideas and opinions than a close-ended question.

Here are some examples of open-ended questions:

- How did that company go from having the most successful product on the market a year ago to filing for bankruptcy today?
- What would success look like for you?
- How do you think we can overcome the lack of motivation within the company?
- Why do we need to change the culture of our company?
- Why is there a need for us to develop a pool of leaders within the company?
- Why should we focus on marketing?
- How did you manage to achieve such spectacular results?

If you are the facilitator or chairperson and you want to get the discussion off to a good start, you should consider asking an open-ended question rather than a close-ended one.

Practice asking five open-ended questions on the following topics:

TOPIC	OPEN-ENDED QUESTION
Smart phones	
Word of Mouth	
Convenience Stores	
Wine Consumption	
Hot Springs	

Practice (Meeting/Discussion)

Participants can take turns serving as facilitators. When serving as a facilitator, be sure to choose a timekeeper and a minute taker. Also, practice going through the whole process from WIRO-AG through AI-BRQ and finally a summary. This time, choose one of the decision making methods discussed above and incorporate it into your proceedings.

1. The stock market

2. Silicon Valley

3. Norman Vincent Peale: The trouble with most of us is that we'd rather be ruined by praise than be saved by criticism.

4. Product warranties

5. Focus groups

6. Shared risk

7. Mutual respect

8. Performance measurement

9. Dealing with suppliers

10. Fast food chains

UNIT 39
Non-verbal Cues

A cue, according to the Learner's Dictionary, "is a sign that tells a person to do something" or "something that indicates the nature of what you are seeing, hearing, etc."

If you have just entered the office and you see the boss in the distance, pounding her fist on the table, that may be a cue that she is not so happy!

The big smile that your colleague gives you after you enter the office in the morning is a cue that all is well between the two of you.

At a meeting, the chairperson and the participants have to be alert to both verbal and non-verbal cues. Participants at a meeting will be looking for cues at the beginning of the meeting as to the state of mind of the chairperson. Is she agitated? Is she happy? Is she worried?

The signs or cues or answers to these questions may be written clearly in the face of the chairperson even before she says a word.

If you are the chairperson, therefore, and you want to set a positive tone for a meeting, be sure that you arrive early, greet all who come in warmly.

Open chitchat or banter with some of the early birds can help show that you are in a good mood and that no one needs to be worried about walking on egg shells. Let your open remarks show that you are happy to see the attendees.

Practice (Meeting/Discussion)

Participants can take turns serving as facilitators. When serving as a facilitator, be sure to choose a timekeeper and a minute taker. Also, practice going through the whole process from WIRO-AG through AI-BRQ and finally a summary. This time, choose one of the decision making methods discussed above and incorporate it into your proceedings.

1. Logistics

2. Cruiseship business

3. Rare earth metals

4. Business retaliation

5. Flooding

6. Gaming boom

7. Switching jobs

8. Working on multiple projects

9. Cooking classes

10. Homelessness

UNIT 40
Verbal Cues

Just as human beings communicate through body language, there are certain verbal signals that can alert us as to what is coming. If someone shouts "Help!" or "Danger" or "Watch out," these are all verbal cues that send a powerful message.

During a meeting, we can use verbal cues to signal when we want to state a point, ask a question, give an opinion, or emphasize a point.

These verbal cues are very important in guiding other participants and can contribute to making for a smooth discussion.

One of the most common verbal cues for giving an opinion is:

- ***In my opinion....***

- In my opinion, Tokyo is one of the best cities in the world.
- In my opinion, hard work almost always pays off.
- In my opinion, women make great leaders.

If you know the appropriate verbal cues to use while participating in a meeting, you will contribute greatly towards its success.

But a meeting is not just about sharing opinions. If you want to run a meeting that achieves substantial results, then you want the kind of meeting that applies creativity and critical thinking.

UNIT 41
Asking the Right Questions

I keep six honest serving-men
They taught me all I knew;
Their names are **What** and **Why** and **When**
And **How** and **Where** and **Who**.
I send them over land and sea,
I send them east and west;
But after they have worked for me,
I give them all a rest.

    - Rudyard Kipling

In most cases, when someone says WHAT... or WHY...or WHEN...that is a cue that the person is going to ask a question.

At a meeting there are cues and signals that you can use to indicate that you are asking for an opinion, sharing an opinion, expanding upon a point you have made, complaining about something, agreeing or disagreeing with someone.

Knowing these cues and using them effectively will help you participate effectively in a meeting whether you find yourself in the chairman's seat or as a participant.

We often have to ask questions that help us clarify something that is unclear. We might also ask questions to raise issues of fairness or to broaden or deepen a discussion.

If we want to ask for an opinion, there are various cues we can deploy. Here are some of them:

1. Could you tell me...?	9. What do you think about...?
2. What do you think of...?	10. What's your opinion of/on...?
3. What do you make of...?	11. What are your views on...?
4. Where do you stand on the issue of...?	12. What would you say to...?
5. What would you say about the question/issue of...?	13. What's your position on...?
6. What are your thoughts on...?	14. I was wondering where you stood on the question of...
7. Do you think that...?	15. Can we get your view on...?
8. What's your input on the issue of...?	

Using the cues above, or any others that are appropriate, what questions can you ask about the topics on the following page?

For example,

TOPIC/ISSUE	CUE
Patent	Could you tell me what your views are on the importance of patents today?
Solar power	What do you think about the future of solar power?

Topic	Question
1) Robots	
2) Pension funds	
3) Electronic waste	
4) Casino gambling	
5) Ebooks	
6) Podcasts	
7) Agricultural subsidies	
8) E-commerce	

UNIT 42
Critical Thinking is Critical

Businesses make numerous decisions everyday. An accumulation of good decisions is likely to translate into success for the business over time. On the other hand, a succession of bad decisions may even lead to the demise of a company.

Executives make big decisions and are often rewarded for the risks they take in doing so. Everyday employees, as it turns, also make many decisions that every company would hope are the right ones.

The pace of change and the global nature of competition means that companies that are able to solve problems and provide the most elegant solutions for consumers or clients are the ones that will win the race.

No business has access to limitless resources. Sometimes, there is not enough money; sometimes there is not enough time; sometimes there is not enough skill; sometimes there is not enough technology; sometimes there is not enough...the list goes on.

And yet, decisions have to be made.

In such an environment, the quality of one's thinking becomes an important differentiating element.

When you are invited to a meeting, you are expected to participate. If you are part of an organization, it means that someone recognizes your skills and your potential to contribute to your organization.

According to a survey done by the American Management Association, "Workers these days "lack communication, collaboration, critical thinking and creative skills" (Harry Bradford, American Workers Lack Common Sense Skills.... www.huffingtonpost.com). In another study, "When more than 400 senior HR professionals were asked in a survey to name the most important skill their employees will need in the next five years, critical thinking ranked the highest -- surpassing innovation or the application of information technology" (Judy Chartrand, Heather Ishikawa, & Scott Flander, Critical Thinking Means Business, 2011).

The rapid pace of business often requires that employees at all levels make decisions quickly. "Good decisions require focusing on the most relevant information, asking the right questions, and separating reliable facts from false assumptions -- all elements of critical thinking" (Chartrand, Ishikawa & Flanders 2011).

What is critical thinking anyway? The word "critical," according to Merriam Webster, expresses "criticism or disapproval," relates to "the judgments of critics about books, movies, art, etc." This meaning of critical widely known and is negative, leading many people to think of critical thinking as a form of criticism.

There are many factors to consider if you want to be a good critical thinker. A starting point is to look at issues from the acronym:

ABAVECI

ASSUMPTIONS

Critical thinking is about examining our assumptions. When we do that, we can uncover hidden values and take steps to overcome values that do not match with where we want to go in our business. For example, when there is 'dangerous' work to be done, do we assume that it is only a man that can do that kind of job. What if there is a woman with greater skill and experience to handle that job. Would you be willing to give that person a chance?

BIASES

Of a group of Americans surveyed in 13 major cities, 75% said that the food they liked best was hamburgers. In Japan, guess what, the most popular food is sushi. If you go to Italy, it might not surprise you to find out that Italians think that Italian food is the best, or that the French believe French food is the greatest or that Chinese believe that they are the best cooks in the world! Funnily enough, they may all be right because they are speaking from their experience. But maybe, rather than saying that one's country's food is the best, just say you really enjoy your country's food and let's understand that you speak from a place of bias when you begin to make comparisons. We may harbor similar biases for our place of birth, the school we went to, the place we have spent a great deal of time, and groups we have been part of. So, when it comes to hiring someone for an important job, who do we think of first? The best person to do the job, or the person who went to the same school as us? Note that biases can come from any number of sources: social, political, economic, religious, cultural, and otherwise.

AUTHORITY

In business, we rely on all kinds of information to make decisions. Authority is about who is behind the information or the order we are about to execute. We do not judge all sources of information in the same way. If we want reliable scientific information, we would not go looking for it in a tabloid. And even among publications, sometimes there are rankings in terms of the prestige or reliability of the information we get from them. So, we should always pay attention to the authority behind our message or information. This also means that at a meeting, if someone makes an outlandish claim, it should be perfectly correct to ask for the source of the information. This kind of questioning can train everyone to be more careful about the information they extract and the quality that may attach to it.

VIEWPOINTS

Just as we have our own biases, we also have our own viewpoints. Sometimes, our viewpoint is based on experience. At other times, it may be based on hearsay or just simply, an opinion. But we cannot simply dismiss other people's opinions because their ideas are not coming from us. We should be open to other people's opinions and be willing to share our own. Quite often, through the clash of ideas and viewpoints, the most useful insights emerge. This does not mean entertaining every crazy idea, but at least, give each idea a chance and winnow them down through discussions until the best idea stands.

EVIDENCE

Whether you are a facilitator or a meeting participant, participation would mean sharing not only your ideas but also making suggestions or coming to conclusions. Any of these would be better served if they are supported by evidence. If you think an approach would work, is it because you have tried that approach before and seen it work? Evidence of success or failure can bolster any new claims you make. And as mentioned before, what is the nature of the evidence? And what is the source of the evidence? How much evidence is there? Is there evidence of just one instance of success or is there a long track record of success? These are matters that ought to be considered.

Another point to consider is how recent the evidence is. It is possible that something that worked 30 years ago might continue to be relevant, but in making decisions and weighing evidence, it is useful to consider how recent the evidence is and evaluate if this supports the new idea you have in mind. Relevance is another key factor. We have to make sure that the evidence we are presenting really applies to the situation we are talking about. If I want to plant flowers in the tropics and the only examples I get come from the arctic, maybe, those examples are not as useful to me as examples from other tropical regions.

CONSISTENCY

If you want to hire someone to do a job, would you rather have someone who is occasionally successful or someone who has a long pattern of success behind her? Whether in sports or business, consistency breeds confidence. When we know that someone has a record of successful achievement, we are more willing to trust that person to deliver another success for us. Critical thinkers pay attention to consistency, in themselves, in their colleagues, and in partners they deal with. Questions about consistency, therefore, can be expected where meeting participants are looking for a pathway to success.

Paying attention to consistency also means making sure that everyone is using the same definition of a word. Some words have different meanings to different people. Thus, if you are not sure what meaning someone is assigning to a word, there is nothing wrong with seeking clarification. This can save a whole lot of headache in the future.

IMPACT:

Everything we do has an impact. Some decisions affect the decision-maker. Some decisions have an impact on our colleagues while still other decisions may have the greatest impact on clients. Thus, the question of impact cannot be swept aside. How big an impact will thedecision have? Who will be affected by the decision? What is the nature of the impact? Will it be positive or negative? How broad or wide will the impact of our decisions be? How deep, how strong, how effective, or how harmful could our decision be if things don't go well?

Recommended materials for further reading

1. Richard Paul & Linda Elder. *Critical Thinking: Tools for Taking Charge of Your Professional and Personal Life.* Pearson FT Press, 2013.

2. 48 Critical Thinking Questions for Any Content Area. 2017.
   https://www.teachthought.com/critical-thinking/48-critical-thinking-questions-any-content-area/

Thinking about Critical Thinking

Based on the above, in your own words, answer the following questions:

1. What is critical thinking?

2. Who do you know that consistently demonstrates critical thinking skills?

3. Can you think of a time when you should have exercised critical thinking but did not. What happened?

Critical Thinking Behaviors

According to Anne and Charlie Kreitzberg, in the article "The Business Case for Critical Thinking Skills," there are distinct behaviors associated with critical thinking. In other words, if you want to be a critical thinker or improve your critical thinking skills, you can do so.

Here is a list of such behaviors:

1	Asks questions that further understanding
2	Doesn't draw conclusions too hastily
3	Considers all sides of an argument
4	Uses criteria to evaluate information
5	Can "push back" effectively
6	Recognizes other people's agendas
7	Explores multiple perspectives
8	Adjusts assumptions in light of new evidence
9	Understands how conclusions were drawn
10	Identify what's known and what isn't

Which of the above have you done most effectively in the past?

Which of the above would you need to improve?

UNIT 43
Raising the Quality of Discussions

What do you remember about critical thinking? Among the key elements of critical thinking is seeing an issue from different points of view.

When a company decides that everyone should come to work at 7 a.m., this may do wonders for a company's productivity, but is the company the only entity affected by such a decision?

What about the employees?
What about the families of the employees?

By looking at the issue from the point of view of different players, you get a fuller picture that might help you make a better decision. Not surprisingly, many of the tools for business analysis look at different aspects or stages of an issue.

Looking at different facets of an issue can also be useful in helping you contribute to a discussion. For practically any issue, you can have a lot to say if you do not consider the issue from just one aspect but do so from many different perspectives. Apply your critical thinking skills.

Practice (Meeting/Discussion)

One person serves as a facilitator. Try to have a complete discussion, and come to a conclusion on it.

1. Best way to build a company's reputation

2. Intrapreneurship

3. Dealing with deadlines

4. Privacy protection in the age of social media

5. How to control stress

6. Relevance of tourism to your nation's success

7. Advice for bullied students

8. Needs of a fledgling startup

9. Best way to recognize top performers

10. Challenges of teamwork

UNIT 44
Dealing with Meeting Disruptions

The Meeting Facilitator has a responsibility to ensure the flow of the meeting and to deal with any disruptions that might come up. This may require firmness and tact. The facilitator's challenge is to deal with the disruption without embarrassing the perpetrator.

The Devil's Advocate

When we make a suggestion and someone points out a weakness in our idea, it forces us to think harder, and if possible, find ways of strengthening our argument. There are people, however, who simply make a sport of opposing any and every idea with clever questioning and rebuttals that do not advance the discussion.

The Devil's Advocate usually focuses only on the negative and might come up with a string of them. Some facilitators deal with this situation by asking participants who object to an idea to come up with two positive ones before offering their negative viewpoint.

Side Chatters and Jokesters

Humor itself is a wonderful thing if it does not get out of hand. In fact, Professor Steven Rogelberg, of the University of North Carolina at Charlotte (USA), says, "Humor is tuypically the sign of a healthy meeting. If people are feeling good and happy, they're more effective in generating ideas and they're more receptive to ideas" ("The Cure for Bad Meetings" www.economist.com).

The sign of trouble is when the humor so overwhelms the meeting that nothing gets done, and the meeting limps along without the outcomes that participants had come to seek. When a meeting has many participants, it is not uncommon to find some participants having their own chatting session within the meeting.

Besides being rude, this can be distracting to other members of the group and hamper the progress of the meeting. Some facilitators deal with this problem by establishing a set of ground rules before the meeting begins. This might include a reminder of how little time there is for the meeting and the need for everyone to focus on the topic at hand. Other facilitators deal with this situation by asking the person who is doing the chatting a question to refocus their attention on the meeting.

The Longwinded Speaker & Dominator

Some speakers make their points three, four or five times even after everyone has understood what they are saying. This can be a waste of time. A good facilitator will use active listening techniques to assure that the longwinded speaker does not waste everyone's time. The longwinded speaker and the dominator can be like the terminator, shutting down everybody else's voice. He or she wants to be the terminator.

In fairness, the dominator might be smart or at least, in the dominator's mind, no one is smarter. The dominator may also have a strong personality, making it difficult for others to want to confront him or her. If unchecked, the dominator monopolizes the meeting, prevents others from speaking, and might push the group into making a less than desirable decision, simply because no one dared to strongly challenge the dominator.

The facilitator can handle the dominator by:

1) Acknowledging understanding of the dominator's main point and asking for others' opinions.

For example, "That sounds like a good idea. Let's hear what others have to say about it."

"It would be useful to hear everyone's opinion."

"Julia, what do you think about X?"

Use the Dominator's Name

"Michael, before we get too far off tangent, I'd like us to discuss how to...Jennie, please tell us what you think about..."

Practice (Meeting/Discussion)

One person serves as a facilitator. Try to have a complete discussion, and come to a conclusion on it.

1. Corporate social responsibility

2. Dealing with crisis

3. Challenges of working remotely

4. Artificial intelligence

5. Walking the talk

6. Benchmarking

7. Happy talk: boon or bane?

8. Moral hazards

9. Corporate training

10. Operating amid uncertainty

About the Author

Everett Ofori holds an MBA from Heriot-Watt University (Scotland, UK) and a Master of Science, Finance, from the College for Financial Planning, Colorado, USA. He teaches Public Speaking, Management, Marketing, and English for Specific Purposes (Business Writing, Medical Writing, Meeting Facilitation, etc.). Everett has helped hundreds of high school and university students around the world to improve their writing and grades. He has also worked extensively with business executives (including those at the C-level).

Everett has worked with clients/students from the following organizations and more:

• Accenture	• Actelion	• Asahi Kasei Medical
• Asahi Soft Drink Research, Moriya	• Astellas	• Bandai
• Barclays	• Becton Dickinson	• Chugai/Roche Pharmaceutical
• Disney	• ExxonMobil	• Fujitsu
• Gyao	• Goldman Sachs	• Hitachi Automotive
• Hitachi Design	• IIJ (Internet Initiative Japan)	• Johnson & Johnson • (Janssen)
• JP Morgan	• JVCKenwood	• Kistler
• L'Oreal	• McKinsey Japan Mitsubishi (Shoji)	• Moody's
• National Institute of Land and Infrastructure Management, Tsukuba, Japan (NILIM)	• Nomura	• Orix
• PriceWaterHouseCoopers	• Recruit	• Reinsurance Group of America (RGA)
• Sekizenkai Nursing School, Soga Hospital, Shimosoga, Kanagawa	• Sumisho	• Summit Agro International
• Sumitomo	• Suntory	• Toppan Printing
• Tokyo International Business College, Asakusabashi, Tokyo, Japan	• Yahoo	• Yokogawa Meter

Notes

Notes

Notes